Towns and Villa
OF ENGLAND

BURTON JOYCE and BULCOTE

BURTON JOYCE & BULCOTE LOCAL HISTORY SOCIETY

ALAN SUTTON

First published in the United Kingdom in 1993 by
Alan Sutton Publishing Limited
Phoenix Mill · Far Thrupp · Stroud · Gloucestershire

British Library Cataloguing in Publication Data

A catalogue record for this book is available from the British Library

ISBN 0–7509–0599–9

Authors:
Norton Collier, Warwick Edwards, Margaret Exley, Mary Gardiner

Editors:
Margaret Exley, Mary Gardiner

Acknowledgements

We should like to thank Jane Berry for typing the copy, John Gardiner for
drawing the map, Bryan Palmer, Ray Parkinson and Gerry Young for copying
photographs, and John Gardiner and Arthur Holmes for checking the proofs.
Thanks also to the following people who have given us information and
allowed us to use their photographs: Jane Adams, Joan L. Allen, Sally
Ashworth, Burton Joyce Methodist Church Council, Ann Carrington, Cyril
Cragg, Joan Davenport, Yvette Frymann, Rosa Lamport, Peter Millward and
the Scouts, Nottinghamshire County Library Local Studies Department,
Florrie Slater, Edna Watson, Eleanor Wright, Stan Wright and many others.

Typeset in Bembo 11/13.
Typesetting and origination by
Alan Sutton Publishing Limited.
Printed in Great Britain by
Hartnolls Ltd, Bodmin, Cornwall.

Contents

1   Early History   1

2   Expansion of the Villages   5

3   Trades and Traders   21

4   Churches   31

5   Clubs and Societies   45

6   Celebrations   54

7   Notable People   59

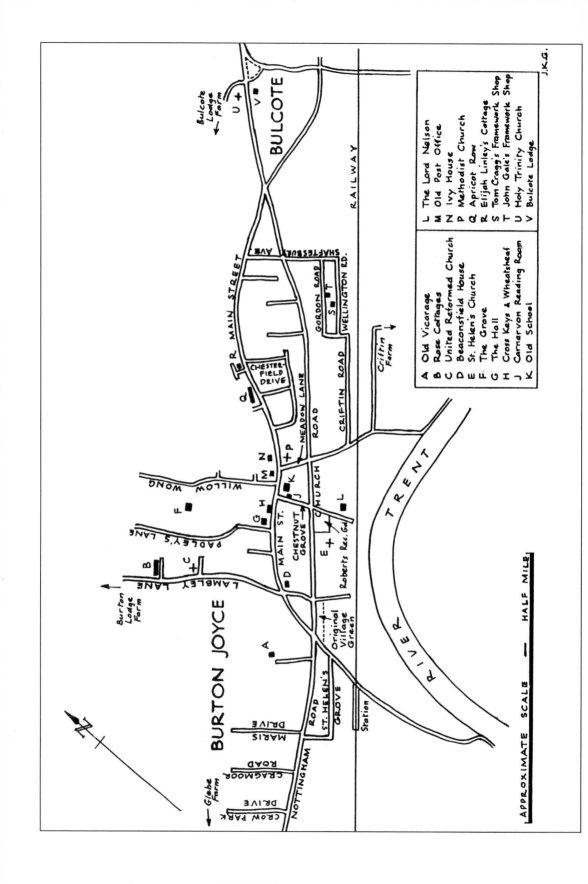

BURTON JOYCE

BULCOTE

Bulcote Lodge Farm

Burton Lodge Farm

Globe Farm

CROW PARK DRIVE
NOTTINGHAM ROAD
CRAGMOOR ROAD
MARIS DRIVE
ST. HELEN'S GROVE
Station
Original Village Green
LAMBLEY LANE
PADLEY'S LANE
WILLOW WONG
Roberts Rec. Gd.
D MAIN ST.
CHESTNUT GROVE
CHURCH ROAD
MEADOW LANE
CHESTERFIELD DRIVE
R MAIN STREET
SHAFTESBURY AVE.
GORDON ROAD
WELLINGTON RD.
GRIFFIN ROAD
Griffin Farm

RAILWAY

RIVER TRENT

A
B
C
F
G H
J
K
E
L
Z M
P
Q
S T
U
V

J.K.G.

A Old Vicarage
B Rose Cottages
C United Reformed Church
D Beaconsfield House
E St. Helen's Church
F. The Grove
G The Hall
H Cross Keys & Wheatsheaf
J Carnarvon Reading Room
K Old School

L The Lord Nelson
M Old Post Office
N Ivy House
P Methodist Church
Q Apricot Row
R Elijah Linley's Cottage
S Tom Cragg's Framework Shop
T John Gale's Framework Shop
U Holy Trinity Church
V Bulcote Lodge

APPROXIMATE SCALE —— HALF MILE

CHAPTER ONE

Early History

Very little remains of 'burh-tun', the fortified farmhouse high on the hill above the present-day village, which we believe was the original Burton. Situated on the ridge that is the parish boundary between the village and Lambley, it would have been in a good strategic position overlooking the Trent valley to the south. It was also at the head of a valley that leads down to the river, where Lambley Lane runs today. Romano-British pottery has been found in this area. Pottery of the first half of the fourth century AD and a coin was also found on the 'Rabbit Bank' (a popular name for the hillside on the north side of Nottingham Road), indicating Roman occupation.

Of the Anglo-Saxon and Danish incursions nothing is known, but Domesday Book tells us that there were settlements here before the Conquest. From this information we are able to estimate that in Burton in 1086 there was a population of about 52. There was also a church and a priest here, and, interestingly, a female slave (*ancilla*), one of only two in the county.

Bulcote, however, was larger at this time with an estimated population of 132, but no church. Both villages had large areas of woodland, as was to be expected since they were both situated within Sherwood Forest, albeit on the southern boundary, which was the River Trent. The names of the inhabitants who lived here in 1086 are not known, but two centuries later some of the villagers are listed in the forest records. In Bulcote these people included 'Lady Lucy of Bulcote and her sisters, heirs of Adam de Sancta Maria, Reginald de Annesley, Elya daughter of William, Agnes widow of Henry son of Florette, Matilda wife of Thomas Barcar and Alan de Schiperton who dwells in Bulcote Wood'. In Burton there were 'Robert and Richard, sons of Ulrich, Robert, son of Ralph Palmer, Robert Burstall, William, son of Osbert, Richard de Burton, William the Reeve and Richard de Jorse'.

THE JOYCE FAMILY

It is not surprising that Richard de Jorse appears in the forest records. He was one of the family who were lords of the manor of Burton for about two hundred years. The name had many variants such as Jorse, Jors, Jorz, Jort, Jortz, Jorce and Joice, until it became Joyce, and eventually the village became known as Burton Joyce. They were a Norman family, originating from a small village called Jort, not far from Falaise in the Calvados region of Normandy. It is said that a Sire de Jort was at the Battle of Hastings. In Domesday Book a Robert de Jorz is listed as holding Wymeswold and Hoton in Leicestershire.

In the time of King John, in about 1200, Geoffrey de Jorz was the keeper of Sherwood Forest. He appears in the records because he annoyed the King in some way and was fined 200 marks (£132) and 4 palfreys. He may have been the first Jorz to settle here, perhaps on top of the hill using the site of the original settlement (medieval as well as the Romano-British pottery was found here), or maybe down in the valley where the later manor was built, with a gatehouse and dovecote, almost certainly on a site at the bottom of Lambley Lane. Here was the centre of the medieval village, with the manor to the west, the church to the east and the village green to the south.

The first concrete evidence of the Jorz connection was in 1235, when Geoffrey, probably the son of the keeper of the forest, was recorded as having a knight's fee (land held from an overlord) in Burton. Richard, Geoffrey's son, inherited the fee. He held the office of verderer in Sherwood and was very much involved in forest affairs, as were many of his descendants. Richard had at least six sons. The eldest, Robert, inherited the fee. The others joined the Dominican Order of Friars, some of them becoming eminent in the order. One, Thomas, reached great heights. After rising in the hierarchy of the

The site of the medieval village

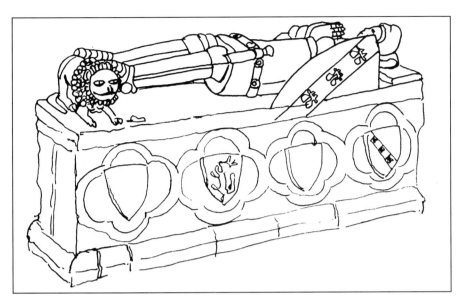

Sir Robert de Jorz's tomb

Dominican Order in England, he entered the service of Edward I and was finally, with the king's help, created a cardinal. His elevation had much influence over the fortunes of the rest of the family. On 11 April 1303 King Edward stayed a night in Burton, no doubt at the Jorz manor, and it is very likely that Thomas was with him. Two of his brothers, Walter and Roland, became successive Archbishops of Armagh, many of the younger members of the family received benefices into vicarages, and in 1307 'Robert, brother of Thomas the Cardinal, was to have in the King's hay at Bestwood and in the wood at Mansfield, 20 oaks fit for timber of the King's gift'. That amount of timber suggests that its use was for building. Perhaps it was needed for extending Robert's manor or the church, or both. For about forty years the Jorz family were prominent in local affairs, holding positions such as verderer, coroner, knight of the shire (member of parliament) and in 1331 Sheriff of Nottingham. This latter appointment was possibly held by Sir Robert de Jorz, whose effigy, a knight in armour, lies in St Helen's church. Little is known of his descendants during the next fifty years, and the direct line finally died out in 1403.

THE LATER MANOR

The fate of the manor is rather obscure for the next few years. Other descendants unsuccessfully made their claims and eventually it was acquired by the Stapletons, a powerful Yorkshire family who were well settled here by

An effigy of Sir Brian Stapleton

the turn of the sixteenth century and were living in the manor house. Sir Brian Stapleton, who died in 1550, is buried in St Helen's church. The alabaster slab from the top of his tomb survives and bears an incised effigy of Stapleton depicted in full armour. This is particularly interesting because his will survives in which he bequeaths his armour to his son, naming the different parts: 'jackes (leather jackets worn underneath), salletes (helmets), splentes (for under-arm protection), almen revettes (light armour from Germany made with moveable rivets) and Legges harnesses'. All of his armour and his 'bowes, arrowes or sheffe of arrowes, haylles, standerds, and any other harness that belongeth to warre' were kept in his 'armye room'.

The manor eventually came into the hands of Sir Michael Stanhope, who had already received the advowson of St Helen's church (then dedicated to St Oswald) after the dissolution of Shelford Priory across the river. From this time there was no resident lord of the manor in Burton Joyce. The Stanhopes settled at Shelford, and it remained their chief seat until it was burned down by the Parliamentarians in the Civil War the following century. The descendants of Stanhope became the Earls of Chesterfield and for the next four hundred years most of the village was to be part of the vast estates subsequently acquired by this powerful family. The medieval manor house gradually decayed and today there is nothing to show of its former grandeur; we cannot even plot its position with any certainty.

CHAPTER TWO

Expansion of the Villages

The earliest existing map of Burton Joyce and Bulcote is one of Sherwood Forest in 1609, now in the Public Record Office. Although we cannot be entirely sure of its accuracy, it shows Burton Joyce to consist of Main Street, Lambley Lane and Meadow Lane. Lambley Lane linked up with the road to Nottingham and a track led towards Bulcote. Meadow Lane is not shown as extending as far as the river bank but must have done so, at least by the mid-seventeenth century, as it was part of the old road to Newark from Nottingham, via Hazelford Ferry, as shown in Ogilvy's map of 1675.

About 35 houses were scattered around these roads, together with the church. The population at this time, calculated from baptisms, Hearth Tax returns and Visitation returns, was about 145. In the next two centuries the village grew only very slowly: the population when official census records began in 1801 was 447, and much of this increase probably occurred during the last few decades, which saw a rapid rise in population throughout the country. Sanderson's map of 'Twenty Miles around Mansfield', made between 1830 and 1834, though on a small scale, shows very little change from 1609.

Meadow Lane, before the bypass was built, showing The Manor House and a cottage

Chestnut Grove, early 1900s

Chestnut Grove had been developed, the first part of Willow Wong is shown and a few cottages had appeared along the road to Bulcote.

The enclosure of the open fields in 1769 had little effect on the layout of the village, as it was chiefly the fields surrounding the centre that were involved. However, this was followed by the building of the outlying farms such as Criftin Farm, Bulcote Lodge Farm and, later, Glebe Farm, situated among their own fields, which had by then been consolidated.

By 1841 there were still only 147 houses in Burton Joyce. The population remained stable during the next two decades at just under 700. This was in spite of the opening of the Nottingham to Lincoln branch of the Midland Railway in 1846. As was common at this time, the station was built at the extreme edge of the village along the lane leading to Stoke Bardolph. Apparently the landlord of the Lord Nelson objected to the station being built near his property, so it was (and still is) sited a good half mile from the centre of the village.

Until the late eighteenth century the village had been an almost entirely agricultural community, with only a few trades such as boatman on the river or blacksmith. For women domestic service was the only opportunity. The introduction at this time of the framework knitting industry was an important development that caused the first notable expansion of the village. Small workshops housing several frames were built alongside some cottages, new cottages were built along Main Street, old cottages were adapted to allow for the rented frames and a few rows of cottages, with big windows suitable for workers renting frames, were built, especially Rose Cottages (Top Row) and

The signal-box and hand-operated crossing gates at Burton Joyce station. The line opened in 1846

Apricot Row, *c.* 1927. These cottages were also once known as Hemington's Row, but apricots once grew on the cottage walls

Brookside Cottages (Bottom Row) off Lambley Lane, and Apricot Row on Main Street. Over a hundred were employed as framework knitters – over a seventh of the population, not counting allied jobs such as seamers and winders. With the influx of framework knitters came a strong surge of Methodism, which resulted in the building of a chapel on Willow Wong in 1823. Later on, in 1869, a Congregational chapel, now the United Reformed church, was built in Lambley Lane from an endowment given by Samuel Milne, a local property developer.

It was not until the last quarter of the nineteenth century, however, that the village really began to expand. The first impetus came from the entrepreneurial schemes promoted by a newcomer to the village, Harry Webster Roberts. Roberts married into a local family, the Alveys, and, acquiring land from them, formed the Burton Joyce Co-operative Land and Building Society Ltd, of which he and the vicar, the Revd R.W. Thompson, were prominent members. They began to develop land in the south-east of the village, attracting Nottingham businessmen by then able to commute owing to the opening of the railway. The first large-scale Ordnance Survey map of 1885 shows that the new roads (later to become Crifton Road, Gordon Road, Wellington Road and Shaftesbury Avenue) were already laid out, and the first houses at the corner of Meadow Lane and Criftin Road (modern spelling) had appeared. A good mixture of large and medium-sized houses had also been built.

Until this time most of the land in the village remained in the ownership of the lords of the manor, the Earls of Chesterfield. In 1871 the land was passed by the female line to the Earls of Carnarvon who, though generous benefactors to the village, especially St Helen's church, were willing to sell

Gordon Road before the First World War

Shaftesbury Avenue, looking towards the village before the bypass was built

land for development. The 'Building Society' purchased land between Station Road and Nottingham Road. The success of their first venture had encouraged them, so they offered seventeen plots for sale on what became St Helen's Grove, which was very handy for the station. Land sold at 2s. 7d. per sq. yd, which included road costs and legal fees. The plots sold quickly. Only five were built on before the end of the century, but these new properties included some fine large houses.

Main Street, looking from the Bulcote end, before 1908 when the Methodist church was built

Semi-detached houses built along the south side of Main Street, around the turn of the century

Further building took place at the other end of the village prior to the First World War. The south side of Main Street had yet to be built on, but then a group of semi-detached houses was constructed, and Chesterfield Drive was built opposite Apricot Row on more land sold by the then Earl of Carnarvon.

The centre of the village was little changed until after the Second World War. The first school had been built in 1850 on land given by the Earl of

'The Building Land': the development of Chesterfield Drive. Apricot Row is in the background

Main Street, looking towards Bulcote, 1908

The village centre, *c.* 1908. The building on the far corner (left of centre) was the post office

The village centre, 7 May 1915. Right to left: the hut used for Scouts and for many other purposes, Count's shop at the end of Wheatsheaf Row, the old Wheatsheaf, the Cross Keys and the chimneys of The Hall in the distance

The approach to Burton Joyce from Nottingham, *c.* 1900

Chesterfield, and when this was quickly outgrown he gave land next to it for the present 'old' school building, opened in 1867. The first Wesleyan church in Willow Wong was replaced in 1907 by today's building, and photographs taken from the tower at that time give us an excellent idea of the village centre and Main Street. Another clear picture of Main Street in 1915, with the two public houses side by side, is given in the postcard of the 'Bantams' marching through Burton Joyce.

The approach to the village from Nottingham had also changed very little. A photograph at the beginning of this century shows the unsurfaced road passing what is now the 'paper shop' and bending round into the bottom of Lambley Lane. Station Road, still undeveloped, goes off to the right and ahead is a road past Church Farm to the church itself. A few houses were built on the right just before Station Road.

With the improvements in transport, including the invention of the motor car, more and more people were able to commute to villages outside the city and Burton Joyce continued its slow expansion. Houses appeared along Station Road, up Lambley Lane and along the 'Rabbit Bank'. By the time of the 1913 Ordnance Survey map the road between Main Street and Lambley Lane had been built, and in 1921 the war memorial was erected on land formerly belonging to Brett's Farm, where in earlier times village sports were held. Crow Park Drive and Cragmoor Road were developed by the builders Cragg and Moore on land that had been used as a bowling green, a cricket pitch and a rifle range, as well as the tennis club, which is the only one to have survived.

A cottage, now The Paper Shop, from the entrance to Station Road, early 1900s

A house on Nottingham Road, pre-1914

The dedication of the war
memorial, 1921

The 'bypass' (Church Road), *c.* 1939

The major development of the inter-war years was the least happy, however. This was the building of the so-called 'bypass', officially Church Road, which, intended to divert traffic from Main Street, has had the effect of bisecting the village, especially now that the traffic it carries is very heavy. However, when it was opened in 1931 it was considered an improvement, and under the heading 'Our Church on the New Road' the vicar, the Revd F.E. Bury, wrote:

> The new road, now finished, brings our beautiful Parish Church out from its hiding place. It always has seemed to me unaccountable, that so many of our Churches have been put where people often have great difficulty in finding them; sometimes necessitating a notice, to the effect that you have to go down a little winding lane and look behind some trees and you will find it. Our Church stands now where people can see it; it is much easier of access, and ought to be much better attended.

Modern traffic conditions have unfortunately destroyed Mr Bury's hopes of easier access to the church, and ribbon development along both sides has helped to make crossing the bypass a serious problem.

Despite all of these developments, in the years before the Second World War Burton Joyce remained a country village, separated by fields from Gedling and a popular place for outings from Nottingham. The hillside north of the

Ivy House and Ivy Cottages, Bulcote, pre-1924

The destruction of the old village centre, 1960s. The Hall, old Wheatsheaf, Rosary Tea Gardens and the old post office have gone

village had only a scattering of buildings and, mainly thanks to the Corporation Sewage Farm at Stoke Bardolph, the riverside has remained open. The 1960s saw the final obliteration of open fields within the centre of the village when Fox Hill was opened for building, and at the same time this area was largely destroyed and rebuilt, with the particularly sad loss of The Hall.

The development of Bulcote has been very different. The two villages were linked as one ecclesiastical parish in 1349, but territorially they belonged to different landowners and are now in different administrative districts. The 1609 map shows about two dozen houses including The Manor House and Bulcote Lodge. There were only 22 houses in 1881 and this number had only increased to 35 by 1921. The church has always stood on the hill above the village and the houses clustered around the central crossroads. Despite its proximity to Burton Joyce, Bulcote never became a village of framework knitters, though a few 'stockingers' lived there.

Ivy Cottages, Bulcote, 1928. Mrs Jenny Staples, the wife of the postman, Fred Staples, and her sons are outside the cottage

Bulcote crossroads, pre-1914

Bulcote has always been associated with farming but has become increasingly residential, losing even its public house and shops. The river bends away from the village and the coming of the railway did not provide easier access since there is no station – Burton Joyce and Lowdham stations are both about two miles distant. The building of the bypass was less destructive to Bulcote: it cut the church off from the village, but by taking the through traffic away created a peaceful backwater.

Bulcote crossing with Corporation Cottages beyond, pre-1914

An aerial view of Bulcote Farm buildings

Corporation Cottages, built for Bulcote Farm employees

However, Bulcote was not to remain totally unchanged. In 1901 Nottingham Corporation decided to extend the existing sewage works at Stoke Bardolph and purchased Bulcote Farm. They erected a magnificent set of model farm buildings between the railway and the river, far in advance of most contemporary farm architecture. The cottages erected for the workforce were of an equally high standard. The farm buildings also provided a social centre for Bulcote and were regularly used for meetings and entertainments. Modern development has not left Bulcote unchanged, but fortunately the new housing is on the edge of the village near Burton Joyce, and the old village has remained largely untouched and is now a conservation area.

CHAPTER THREE

Trades and Traders

FARMING

During the nineteenth century the two main trades in Burton Joyce and Bulcote were farming and framework knitting, the latter confined to Burton Joyce. In 1832, according to *Wright's Directory of Nottinghamshire*, there were nine farmers living in Burton Joyce and three in Bulcote. The century that followed saw the disappearance of all but three of these: Glebe Farm and Burton Lodge Farm in Burton Joyce and Bulcote Lodge Farm. The farms in the centre of the village disappeared gradually as the village expanded and were swallowed up as building land.

From the 1881 census it is possible to get a fairly accurate idea of the farms existing within the village area. Mark Baguley farmed Crow Park Farm with 176 acres. The farmhouse still exists, on the corner of Lambley Lane and Main Street, and the barn is now a doctor's surgery. In 1920, when there was a major auction sale of farming land, it was described as a 106 acre dairy farm and sold to a Mr Frettingham for £6,300. In 1881 Church Farm consisted of

Lambley Lane and Crow Park Farm. Brett's Home Field was on the left

Church Farm

100 acres and was farmed by Isaac Mosley, who employed three men, but at the auction of 1920 only the farmhouse and farm buildings with an acre of land remained. The house has now been demolished and a block of maisonettes built in its place. As its name suggests it was very near the church, and part of the land was used for the cemetery. In 1881 Brett's Farm was much larger, having 310 acres. Its fate is dealt with later (p. 65). Hannah Cheshire, a widow, occupied the 50 acre Criftin Farm and was described as a

Church Farm house up for sale

coal merchant. The coal was brought by barge along the Trent. This farm was swallowed up in the Corporation Farm and the buildings demolished comparatively recently.

There were also the trades associated with farming, such as the blacksmith. His 'shop' is still in the village but has changed use several times and is now a dance studio. In 1832 Joseph Alvey was the blacksmith. He was succeeded by his son Matthew, and in 1853 there were two blacksmiths in the village. Making and repairing wheels was another important trade within a farming community, and in 1832 the wheelwrights in Burton Joyce were J. and W. Seston. By 1853 William Seston had been joined by Jacob Bidgood. John Seston was still listed as a wheelwright and joiner in 1881, together with Bidgood, now aged seventy. John's fifteen-year-old son is described as a framework knitter. One can just imagine the sounds of hammering and hissing as these workmen plied their trade.

Progress and change in the early twentieth century saw the smith give way to the motor engineer, and by 1925 *Kelly's Directory of Nottinghamshire* shows that there were three such works in Burton Joyce: A.R. Atkey, Simpson & Shepherd and Lambley Lane Garage (Crow Park Barn before it became a doctor's surgery). Farming was by this time becoming mechanized. The first tractor to work in Burton Joyce, a G.O. made in Birmingham, operated on Crow Park Farm in 1919. Until then most farming activities employed

The smithy after it became a grocers shop

horses, which kept saddler and harnessmaker Thomas Allcock very busy. He first appears in *Lascelles and Hagar's Directory* of 1848, and according to *Kelly's Directory* was still in business in 1900 when he would have been in his seventies. His son joined the business, but they were the last of the trade to work in the village. In 1928 the motor engineers Gosling and Vickers appeared in the village. Their business still survives today. Also in *Kelly's Directory*, John Sherwin's garage is listed, but his business folded in the 1970s and the site is now a prestigious residential development.

FRAMEWORK KNITTING

The second main trade in the village in the nineteenth century was framework knitting. The invention of the knitting machine or, as it is more commonly called, the stocking frame owed its origin, it is believed, to William Lee of Calverton, who lived only a few miles from Burton Joyce. The first mention of a framework knitter in the village was in the 1841 census, which records the presence of 96 knitters. *Wright's Directory* of 1853 mentions only Richard Wood, who presumably employed a few workmen, described in the census as 'lodgers'.

The directories listed only the knitters who employed a few workmen, many of whom had their own workshops. These included William Cragg,

Dolly Brown outside 63 Main Street, where Edward Barrowcliffe had a shop

John Gale's workshop, Wellington Road

whose great-grandson Cyril, now in his eighties, still lives in the village, and Edward Barrowcliffe, Cyril's maternal great-grandfather, whose 'shop' was at 63 Main Street. He, with his wife, also sold home-made sweets and cakes. By 1869 John Gale, another famous knitter, started his career as a lodger and apprentice with Barrowcliffe, but by 1871 had set up his own workshop in Wellington Road. He later extended this to house about fourteen frames. He achieved fame at the Paris Exhibition of 1900 where his work was awarded a diploma, still in the possession of his family. His workshop had a large area of small-paned windows, which were essential to obtain the maximum light for such intricate work. This was particularly necessary in Burton Joyce as much of the work was in black silk for the luxury trade. The light was enhanced by the use of a special diffuser, made by shining light through a round bottle containing water with hydrochloric, sulphuric or nitric acid in it. The building is now a private garage.

Ivy House on Main Street had its own frame shop where the Cragg family worked. Most of the frames in the village were rented from large firms in Nottingham such as I. & R. Morley, whose collectors, known as bag hosiers or bag men, would come round the villages collecting the finished goods and supplying further raw materials. They were also responsible for quality control and paying the knitters, and there was much friction in connection with these two matters!

Ivy House, Burton Joyce, which retains its long window to light the knitters' workshop

Tom Cragg's house and workshop,
Wellington Road

Surgical hosiery was a speciality of Burton Joyce. Tom Cragg, who also had a workshop in Wellington Road, and Frederick Cragg, at the corner of Tim Lane and Main Street, made such items. When the industry as a whole began to decline as a result of the invention of machines for lace and hosiery, the elastic bandage was the last part of the industry to be mechanized.

Giving evidence to the commission that was set up to investigate working conditions in the industry in 1844, Thomas Atkin of Burton Joyce stated that there were 'somewhere about 100' frames in the village, and there were 'two or three small bagmen (knitters who owned and rented out frames); One has about 14 or 15 frames, another has about 12, and there may be one or two have less.' Some of the main complaints in Burton Joyce were that the bag men would continually change their requirements with regard to size and width, without offering extra pay, that knitters were kept short of work and that some of the knitters were not being paid 'the warehouse prices'. Atkin stated that the average wage paid in the village varied 'From about 6s. to 9s. first-hand'. When asked whether there were any public schools in the village he said, 'No, we want one very badly.' As regards Sunday Schools he replied, 'Yes, the Church and the Methodist.'

At its height the framework knitting industry, with its subsidiary occupations such as winders and seamers, employed over a hundred people. There were a large number of knitters' cottages in Burton Joyce, in particular Rose Cottages, a whole row of tiny cottages, many of which contained a frame. The 'thump and bang' of the frames must have been heard all over the

Rose Cottages, Lambley Lane

The Lord Nelson public house

village, and were described by Mr H.W. Roberts, benefactor of the village, as 'the music of the handframe knitter'. Some worked only part-time at the frames, such as Elijah Linley the parish clerk, but in other cases the whole family was involved.

Until very recently Burton Joyce was an almost self-sufficient village with a wide variety of small traders, including butchers, joiners, boot repairers, drapers, grocers, fruiterers, coal merchants, painters, builders and carriers. For instance in 1885, according to *White's Directory*, there were three butchers: Leslie Goodall, Henry Greaves and John Barnes who was also the landlord (victualler) of The Lord Nelson, one of the three inns in the village. All three inns are still in business today, the other two being the Cross Keys and the Wheatsheaf. John Barnes bought his animals in the market and kept them in a paddock, before slaughtering them at the back of his shop and selling the meat during the week.

Various branches of the Slater family were active in the village in the early part of this century as farmers, butchers and publicans, but the best known is Edward Slater who became a wheelwright, joiner and undertaker. Some of the furniture he made remains in the village, and his workshop and many of his tools still survive.

The former smithy became a grocer's shop in the early twentieth century. It was first kept by D. & E. Laurie, and later by W.H. Wells. A number of receipts were found recently during repairs to the roof. Mr Wells was evidently an important man in the local community and, when he died suddenly in September 1931, there were two obituaries in the parish magazine, one from the vicar and the other from the British Legion, of which he was the local

Edward Slater (right) and a
summerhouse he built

A receipt from Wells's grocers
shop

MAIN STREET,   4786
BURTON JOYCE, *Oct 29*   192_

Mrs Coney

Bought
of   **W. H. WELLS,**

Family Grocer & Provision Dealer.

sm Tomatoes			5½
Bacon			5
Coal			8
2 choc			3

Mr and Mrs Thompson of The Rosary Tea
Gardens

treasurer. Wells had served in the army from 1892 to 1912 in India, Malta and
Egypt, becoming quartermaster sergeant and re-enlisting during the First World
War. He belonged to the Methodist church and had been secretary of the
Soldiers' Christian Association while in the army. His funeral filled the church,
and both the Methodist minister and the vicar took part. Although there have
been shops from time to time in Bulcote there was then no grocer, but orders
could be left at Wells's shop and were delivered by his errand boy on a bicycle.

One of the attractions of the village was the Rosary Tea Gardens. In 1885
they were owned by Mrs Goodall, but by 1900 they had been taken over by
the three Miss Taylors

who lived in the house adjoining the gardens. They made all their own
cakes and served fruit, salads and sandwiches. There were swings in the
orchard and a covered verandah for shelter in the rain, and often the
Salvation Army band came to play.

They were very popular with the many visitors who travelled out from
Nottingham in their leisure time at the beginning of this century. Mr and
Mrs Thompson took over the tea gardens from the Taylors just before the
Second World War.

Chapter Four

Churches

St Helen's Church

There is a chapter on St Helen's church in *Burton Joyce & Bulcote, Studies in the History of Two Trent Valley Villages* (published by the History Group in 1979). For this reason it is not proposed to devote space here to the early history, but rather to look at the social life of the church, drawing on information from early editions of the parish magazine. These publications have survived from two periods: 1885–95 and 1923–34. The magazine was begun by the Revd Reginald W. Thompson (see p. 85) and in that first edition classes and meetings are listed. These included the Mothers' Meeting at 7.00 p.m. and choir practice at 8.00 p.m. on Mondays. The Juvenile Branch of the Church of England Temperance Society met on alternate Wednesdays at 5.30 p.m. and the Girls' Friendly Society classes were on

St Helen's church, 1930s

Saturdays at 5.00 p.m. These meetings were all held in the schoolroom. The GFS also met at the vicarage on Mondays at 7.30 p.m. The Sunday School opened at 9.45 a.m. and 2.15 p.m. There was also a library open on alternate Wednesdays at 4 p.m. Subsequent magazines mentioned a Communicants' Guild, the Men's Institute and two bible classes, one for men and the other for young women. They also show that the church supported the Church Missionary Society, as it still does today.

Nearly thirty years later, when the magazine was issued again after an interval during the war, there was no Temperance Society and no Mothers' Meetings (the latter probably because the Women's Institute had been formed by this time). However the GFS and bible classes were still flourishing, as was the library.

The Choir

In the beginning there was no shortage of boys for the choir, but the first parish magazine put in a plea that more bass and tenor voices were wanted. A set of rules was hung up in the choir vestry under the tower. There was some trouble over rule 5, as an entry in the vestry book for May 1898 shows. It said that the choir men complained on the subject of rule 5 'intimating very distinctly that unless rule 5 were enforced their own position w'd become untenable and they would be obliged to resign'. Later 'The Vicar undertook to ask Mr. Sansome to accept the initial authority to decide <u>when</u> in the case of any choir-boy the rule 5 became applicable, and in consequence to request his retirement accordingly.' In June four boys were disqualified 'till such time as he shall be qualified, with advantage to himself and to the choir to resume his place in the choir'.

Each year there was a choir excursion, which seemed to be open to anyone who wished to go. In September 1885 the magazine recorded:

We may look upon our Choir Excursion this year as having been a great success. At half-past seven in the morning the platform of the Railway Station presented a very animated appearance. As it was the last cheap trip to Cleethorpes for the season, about two hundred of our parishioners were assembled to avail themselves of a run to the sea-side. Two carriages being reserved for the choir, we were soon speeding on our way, gathering additional numbers at Lowdham and Thurgarton . . . [He then goes on to say how most of the passengers alighted at Grimsby and walked through the docks and continues] . . . A walk along the sands brought us to Cleethorpes, where arrangements were made for dinner at the Dolphin Hotel. We are bound to say that everything was

St. Helen's Church Choir.

BURTON JOYCE.

✝

Member's Name _____

✝

RULES.

1—All boys belonging to the Choir must attend practice regularly, unless a proper and reasonable excuse is given.

2—No talking, whispering, laughing, or misbehaviour of any kind will be allowed, either in the Tower or Church at any time.

3—Practice will be held on Wednesday evening at 8-15 p.m., or at any other time as may be arranged.

4—Boys will be paid for practice at the rate of 2/- per quarter subject to Rule No. 1.

5—If at any time a voice is found to be unsuitable to the Choir the boy may be asked to resign.

6—Any boy not obeying the above Rules will be liable to be dismissed from the Choir.

7—In all cases of resignation from whatever cause, or dismissal, the Card of Rules must be returned for certificate of character.

REGINALD W THOMPSON, Vicar.

GEORGE HURST, }
THOMAS MARSH, } Churchwardens

ARTHUR JOHNSON, PRINTER, NOTTM

St Helen's church choir rules

served in very good style. We had a large, cheerful room, good attendance and excellent fare, added to which there was the presence of some ladies amongst us this year, which we hope may be continued in the future. In the afternoon we all broke up into little parties and went various ways. For many the attractions of the sands and donkey-riding seemed to have great charms, while some enjoyed the less exciting movement of sailing on the sea. On walking near the pier we so continually met some of our fellow-parishioners that but for the different surroundings we might have fancied ourselves still in Burton Joyce. After tea and another short time for strolling about we repaired to the Railway Station, and in due time started on our way homeward, where we were safely landed at half-past eleven, every one feeling that the day had been a very enjoyable one.

Each year an appeal was made for funds for the choir excursion and the Whitsun collections were usually used for this purpose. Sometimes they went to Cleethorpes, sometimes to Skegness. During the General Strike in 1926, 'owing to the absence of railway facilities in consequence of the coal stoppage', they had to postpone their outing to Skegness but had a successful time later. In the 1920s and '30s Skegness was the most popular venue with the choir boys, as this account in the July 1929 edition of the magazine makes clear. This was obviously written by a choir member, perhaps Mr John Brammer, their leader and trainer, who died in December 1929.

And so it is when our good Churchwardens ask the choir 'where do you want to go for your outing?' Skegness we say. And Skegness it is, and will be I think, for Skegness is limitless in its attraction to all of us. A party of thirty-three, or was it thirty-four, or was it thirty-one. Bother the boys, they do move about so in the carriage I can't count them. Anyway, we all went, and all included the Vicar and Mrs Bury, who were absolutely charmed with Nottingham-by-the-Sea . . . And then, off we went, the boating lake an 'easy first' attraction. We won gorgeous packets of sweets – but oh! at what cost – at putting balls into holes, we threw darts and shot corks from rifles and waggled handles . . . We climbed a dizzy tower and shot down a slippery slope into a slippery basin. Hush, don't tell, but they do say the basin was nearly broken by a nearly reverend and weighty member of our party . . . All too soon came the hurry to the station and the comfortable journey home, during which we sang Mr J.C. Woodsend's health and all too joined in the regret that we felt that other Churchwardens Messrs. Hearnshaw and Scott, were unable to enjoy the outing with us.

They earned their annual treat; this is what the vicar thought of the choir in 1932:

> The singing in Church and the wonderful combination of the Choir and organ are most noticeable, and quite a number of visitors have remarked on this in most complimentary terms. Our Church Choir, they say, has quite a distinctive quality that is not very prevalent in Village Churches.

The Bible Classes and St Helen's Tennis Club

Although there were thriving bible classes, in both Mr Thompson's and Mr Bury's day, they are mentioned infrequently in the parish magazine. In 1925 the girls' bible class arranged a social evening with an 'attractive programme' comprising songs, recitations, a play and dancing: a full evening of entertainment for a shilling, including refreshments! It was in 1933, during Mr Bury's time, that the Tennis Club was formed, as follows:

> The St. Helen's Tennis Club originated through the Young Men's Bible Class, and commenced on Easter Monday of this year. It has been a very jolly and profitable season, and has been the means of many, happy friendships. We played a delightful match against the St. Jude's Tennis

St Helen's choir, 1932. The vicar (centre) is the Revd Fenton Ernest Bury (who so much enjoyed 'Nottingham-by-the-Sea!'). He was vicar from December 1928 to November 1934, when he died suddenly in his sleep, aged seventy

Some members of St Helen's choir, 1952. By this time there were lady members. Left to right: Roland Dawes, Joan Butler (now Bolton), Ivy Jukes, Lawrence Butler, John Barnes. The vicar (right) is Canon Morlais Williams. Bishop Barry is in the background

The bible class, c. 1937

Club from Mapperley, on Saturday, Sept. 2nd, and hope to fix up several similar matches, with other clubs, next spring. A fitting conclusion to the season was a Squash Supper and Social held at the vicarage from 8.30 to 11.30, including a firework display, games and a presentation to Mr. & Mrs. Bury for their kindness and encouragement.

The Mothers' Union (November 1931 Magazine)

In the parish magazine of November 1931 the following report was made:

On Tuesday, October 13th, a branch of the Mothers' Union was formed in Burton Joyce and Bulcote. There was quite a good gathering at the Vicarage, and the meeting was addressed by Mrs. Hales, wife of the Rural Dean, and by Mrs. Pearson, of Lowdham. It was decided to hold a meeting on the second Tuesday in each month at 3 p.m. The next meeting will therefore be on Nov. 10th. We give a very warm welcome to all who would care to come and join us. The Mothers' Union is the finest organisation in the Church of England, and every woman belonging to the Church of England should become a member of it.

The Tennis Club at the vicarage, 1933. The Revd F.E. Bury is towards the left of the back row

For many years the Mothers' Union has had a choir, which is still thriving today.

Apart from the social life of the church the magazines also mention any refurbishment of the building. One such matter came up in 1929 in a Church Council meeting when 'complaints having been made as to the inadequate lighting of the Church, it was decided to obtain estimates and designs to introduce "inverted" gas burners in the place of the present upright type'. It was decided to replace the lights with inverted Bray burners. These were installed by the following March, when it was reported that they gave 'far better light'.

Another interesting announcement occurred in an issue of 1887:

Our parish has lately been attached to a new Rural Deanery formed partly out of the overgrown Deanery of Nottingham and partly out of

The Mothers' Union choir, *c.* 1951

The interior of St Helen's church, 1920s. Both 'upright' burners and some splendid candlesticks are in use

that of Southwell. The Bishop has appointed as our first Rural Dean, the Rev. Allan G.M. Meugens, Rector of Carlton, a gentleman well known to us for the interesting and successful work he gave to Burton Joyce during the time he was its Vicar.

Allan George Munro Meugens came to Burton Joyce as Vicar in 1878 and left in 1883 to become the first rector of the newly built church of St Paul, Carlton-in-the-Willows.

Although today St Helen's does not run the social life of the village as it did a hundred years ago, it is still a thriving concern. The year of 1993 marks another chapter in its history with the opening of the new Church Centre on the south side. This is a graceful building, which tones in beautifully with the church and carries on the tradition of improvements that have taken place over the centuries.

HOLY TRINITY, BULCOTE
The Medieval Church

There is no mention of a church at Bulcote in Domesday Book. It is thought that it was probably founded as a manorial chapel within the parish of Burton

Joyce by the Sancta Maria family, who were lords of Bulcote in the thirteenth century. Records tell us that Adam Sancta Maria, who lived here in the first half of the century, gave the advowson of Holy Trinity church (the right to appoint a clergyman to a living), together with lands at Bulcote, to the Abbot and convent of Welbeck for the sake of the souls of his first wife, Alice, and his son, Bartholomew. It remained with Welbeck until it was surrendered to the Prior and convent of Shelford in exchange for the advowson of Kelham. In 1349 both Burton Joyce and Bulcote churches were appropriated by Shelford Priory, and the document accompanying this transaction states that the vicar 'shall find at his own costs and charges one able Chaplain to celebrate Divine Service in the Chapel of Bulcoate'. On the dissolution of the priory in 1536 both churches were appropriated by Sir Michael Stanhope. Bulcote church has been dedicated to Holy Trinity since at least the seventeenth century.

Survival and Upkeep

We know very little of the church in the next few hundred years, except for a few 'snippets' in the records of the Archdeacon's Court. If it was found that the church was not in good repair or was lacking in the necessary equipment at the 'visitations' of the archdeacon or his official, the churchwardens were summoned to the court and ordered to put the matter right. As can be seen from the following extracts, Holy Trinity has not always been as well maintained as it is today. In 1592 Sir Thomas Stanhope is mentioned because 'the Chancel at Bulcote is presented to bee decaid in his defaulte'. In November 1602 the wardens of Bulcote were summoned because 'the belfrie is out of repair'. Only one warden, Thomas Burrage, was present and he was ordered to appear with his colleague within fifteen days. In December they were still being ordered to repair 'the bell house of theire church before St John the Baptists day'. They were summoned again the following October (it doesn't say why but it was probably for the same offence). Then, because they did not appear at the court, they received the ultimate punishment: excommunication! The church was again out of repair in 1683. In May 1718 the churchwardens were 'admonished to repair their chancel and chapel in ye roofe, windows, pavement and out walls and especially the south side thereof which if falling must be pull'd down and built up again'. They were ordered to appear at the court in October to report progress. This time they complied with the order and the court was pleased to report that 'ye church and chapell of Bulcote is repaired in every respect according to ye admonition of ye archdeacon'. In 1753 the parsonage house at Bulcote was 'very much out of repair'. Exactly where this house was is not known, but it was probably near the church.

The Collapse and the New Church

About a hundred years later in 1860 the church was in an even worse state. Major Egerton Leigh wrote to the ecclesiastical commissioners saying, 'the church of Bulcote has been closed by order and is falling down and parting in all directions'. He suggested that the cost of rebuilding would be about £900 and said that he had £750 ready to spend immediately. He requested more aid from the commissioners, but to no avail. A year after this, tradition has it, Miss Popplewell, while looking out of her window at Bulcote Lodge opposite, saw the collapse of part of the church. News of this catastrophe appeared in the *Illustrated London News* of 20 July 1861 under the heading 'Country News': 'A few days ago a violent thunderstorm passed over the villages of Lowdham, Carlton, etc. Nottinghamshire, and during the storm the electric fluid struck the parish church of Bulcote, and the building fell to the ground.' The vicar, the Revd John Rolleston, rushed with his camera to record this exciting event.

The old Bulcote church, shortly before its collapse

Miss Maria Popplewell of Bulcote Lodge

It is difficult, looking at the photograph of the tower now, to reconcile its appearance with John Throsby's description in his edition of 'Thoroton's Antiquities' (*The Antiquities of Nottinghamshire* by Robert Thoroton, 1677) of 1796, where he says, 'The Chapel, which is topped like a pidgeon house, has no attractions.' After its collapse the whole building was pulled down and rebuilt in two years in a completely new style and was dedicated in 1862. Of course, even a new church needs refurbishing in time. The parish magazines furnish us with further information as the following extracts show. In 1887 the organ was 'found to be so much in need of repair' and 'one of the stone crosses on the roof was blown down and broken'. A subscription was begun and this was headed by Miss Popplewell, who gave £2. In 1891 the church was thoroughly cleaned and repaired at a cost of £11 16s. 6d. In 1895

The gale on 24th March did serious damage to the roof of Bulcote Church. It is impossible to estimate the harm done till the architect's report has been received, but it is feared that a very serious outlay will be necessary to make the roof safe.

Two months later the repairs were put in hand and this time Miss Popplewell contributed £5.

Bulcote church after its collapse

The new Bulcote church

Nearly thirty years later the 1923 magazine again related:

the work of renovating and cleaning the church has been completed and the result is very satisfactory, the damp spots and patches on the walls are quite obliterated and the interior of the church is now greatly improved. The cost has been defrayed mainly out of the collections in church but also by the aid of a whist drive on Nov. 30th organised by a committee of ladies, viz., Mrs Kraus, Mrs Lockett, Mrs Marshall, Mrs Smith and Mrs Wright. The whist drive was held at the messroom of Bulcote Farm, through the kindness of Mr Stone and the Stoke Farm Committee, and resulted in a very pleasant evening being spent, and a gain to the fund of £5.15s.

The total cost of this work was £70 4s. 0d. and was all paid for by the following July.

The residents of Bulcote are still working hard to keep their church in good repair. Today it is in immaculate condition owing to their continuing hard work in raising money, including interesting events such as their successful village markets on the green. There is certainly no sign of a collapse today.

CHAPTER FIVE

Clubs and Societies

A wide variety of clubs and societies has been formed in Burton Joyce and Bulcote. Some, for unknown reasons, have ceased to function, while others have gone from strength to strength and continue today in the active life of the village.

CRICKET CLUB

Probably one of the earliest clubs was the Burton Joyce Cricket Club, which was founded in 1873. Cricket had evidently been a popular leisure pursuit for many years prior to this date: in 1814 the *Nottingham Journal* reported a match between Burton Joyce and East Bridgford. Alfred Shaw was a

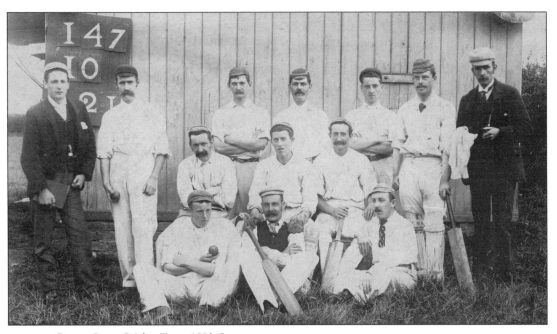

Burton Joyce Cricket Team, 1893–5

renowned member of the club. He went on to play for the Nottinghamshire County CC and for England on their tours of Australia, first in 1877 and later, as captain, in 1881. Having celebrated its golden jubilee in 1923, the club continued until the mid-1920s, when it was succeeded by a combined Burton Joyce and Stoke Bardolph Club, using a ground at Stoke where it continues today.

TENNIS CLUB

At a meeting in 1890 the Burton Joyce Tennis Club was formed. Two courts were made available on ground that had been obtained, and many people were reported to have joined. Little is known of the club during the next fifty years or so, but there was obviously considerable interest in the game since some twenty private courts were known in the village. It was not until 1938 that another club appeared as Cragmoor Tennis Club, with twenty-one members and two courts with a small pavilion, which also housed a dame-school during term time. After a break during the war years the club resumed activities as Burton Joyce Tennis Club. It went on to purchase the grounds and pavilion, add a third court and carry out appropriate resurfacing. With the closure of the school in 1958 and improvements to the pavilion, the club reached the flourishing position that it has maintained since.

A tug o' war at the flower show, 1905

A wheelbarrow race in Brett's Field as part of the sports at the flower show, 1906

FLOWER SHOW

In October 1892 'a meeting was held of gentlemen interested in getting up a Flower Show' in the village in the following year. In due course a committee was formed, subscribers cajoled into providing the necessary finance and plans put in hand for the event on Bank Holiday Monday, 7 August. It was subsequently reported that the show was a great success. Sports and entertainment by the village drum and fife band complemented the display of flowers, fruit and vegetables in a large tent on the Home Field, an area between Lambley Lane and where the war memorial and adjacent buildings are today.

In later years the range of exhibits was extended to include poultry. This was perhaps the influence of a patron, Mr Hearnshaw, who was president of the National Poultry Club. Entries in the poultry section were even made by HRH The Prince of Wales (Edward VIII, later Duke of Windsor), who won prizes on at least two occasions. After the break during the war years an attendance estimate for the 1920 show of 2,800 people indicates that the event was a gala day, not only for Burton Joyce but also for many visitors. Owing to the gradual encroachment of the road and of house building, the show moved indoors in 1927. Since then the show has remained in the relatively new village hall. The year 1993 marked the show's centenary.

FOOTBALL CLUB

A village football team was known to be playing in about 1900. Members of the Men's Institute formed a successor club in 1926, which certainly had a satisfactory first season, recording eight wins and only one loss.

Football team, *c*. 1890. The man with the beard is William Caunt, the lamplighter

BOY SCOUTS AND GIRL GUIDES

In 1909, just one year after the movement was founded, a Boy Scout troop was formed in Burton Joyce with an initial camp at Willow Wong Farm. There followed a comprehensive programme over many years of camps and scouting activities. The year 1914 saw a visit by the movement's founder, General Baden-Powell, an occasion marked, among other events, by the presentation of a suitably inscribed bugle to the troop by Major G.T. Williams. A Wolf Cub pack was added in 1929.

In November 1940 the following report appeared in the *Nottingham Boy Scouts Gazette*:

Patrol Leader Eric Saunders, of 1st Burton Joyce (A.W. Carr's Own Group), has been awarded the Gilt Cross for his prompt and gallant action in stopping a runaway horse at Burton Joyce on August 4th, 1940.

Some Scouts and Guides were marching off to a Church Parade along the main road at Burton Joyce when an unattended horse attached to a milk cart took fright and bolted. The Scouts and Guides were brought to a halt and Saunders leapt at the horse's head and succeeded in turning

The 1st Burton Joyce Scouts at camp, Mablethorpe, 1919. Note the bugles. The Union flag is being held by Cyril Cragg, who joined the troop in 1914 and who is today the oldest surviving scout in the village

Scout patrol leader, Eric Saunders

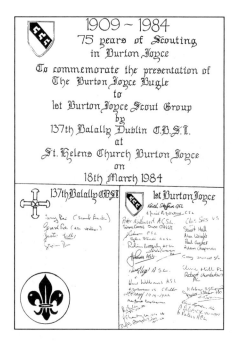

A certificate commemorating the 75th anniversary of Scouting in Burton Joyce

the animal into a side lane. Robson then dashed to the other side of the horse's head and between them the boys brought the horse to a standstill. A large number of children were standing at the corner of the lane watching the parade go by and one small boy on a tricycle was right in the track of the horse. There were only a few inches between the boy and the horse when Saunders made the animal swerve and miss the boy. The County Commissioner is to make the presentations at the Village Hall, Burton Joyce on Sunday, 17th November at 3.30 p.m.

Also at about this time the presentation bugle unaccountably disappeared. However, thanks to the observation of Tony Roe, a Scout leader of Balally, Dublin, who saw and purchased the bugle in an antique shop, it was returned with due ceremony to Burton Joyce in 1984 after an absence of almost forty years, on the occasion of the troop's 75th anniversary.

A Girl Guides company was started in 1925, with the addition of a Brownie pack in the following year.

WOMEN'S INSTITUTE

In 1919 a local branch of the Women's Institute was formed and began to take an active part in village life. In December 1923, after only four years, it

50

A group of Burton Joyce Guides at camp, Walesby, *c.* 1940

Women's Institute group. The trophy is being held by Miss Blagg

Burton Joyce village hall shortly after it was built, 1925

Burton Joyce Amateur Dramatic Society's production of *The Chinese Honeymoon*, village hall, 1929

played a major part in encouraging the scheme to construct a village hall. An immediate financial commitment was made and, during the following couple of years, fund-raising efforts proceeded. The result was that in November 1925 the hall was officially opened. The Women's Institute has maintained a strong membership ever since, so much so that, in order to provide for those who preferred evening meetings, a second group was formed.

DRAMATIC SOCIETY

Many organizations and groups began to make use of the new hall, with concerts, whist drives, Dickens readings and performances by visiting companies. At the end of 1926 Burton Joyce Amateur Dramatic Society was formed. It staged its first production, *The Geisha*, in 1927. The society presented plays until 1929, when it added musical productions to the repertoire. It continued until the outbreak of war, after which it resumed life as the Burton Joyce Players, presenting two productions a year of stage plays and, more recently, a Christmas pantomime, much to the enjoyment of the village children.

CHAPTER SIX

Celebrations

In the April 1887 issue the parish magazine recorded 'Plans for the Queen's Jubilee' and continued:

> Amongst others, a project has started in Burton Joyce for putting up a clock on the outside of our School House . . . It stands to reason that if we have such a clock, one on which we could depend for telling us the time, it should be a really good one . . . a sum of about forty guineas will be required.

The necessary sum was raised by public subscription. Confirmation that the clock was indeed 'a really good one' may be seen in its functioning over one hundred years on. Its life has not been entirely uneventful, for in 1923 the magazine recorded: 'During the War, the clock for some reason or other seemed to be somewhat out of condition and on occasions it seemed to be

Coronation festivities in Burton Joyce, 1953. The 'carnival procession' had to take place in the village hall because of the poor weather

The old school. The clock was installed for Queen Victoria's Jubilee

inclined to strike against striking the correct time.' An appeal follows for subscriptions towards its upkeep and the cost of winding by Mr Caunt at an annual fee of a guinea, 'but there should be some surplus for repairs, etc.'.

The Coronation Day Jubilee entertainments were described as having 'passed off admirably', both at Bulcote and Burton Joyce, as the following extract from the parish magazine shows:

At Bulcote, there was a service in Church, after which all assembled in Mr. Alvey's barn which, on this occasion presented somewhat the appearance of a ball-room, so gaily was it decorated. Here a substantial meal was provided and duly enjoyed. Then, the company adjourned to a field hard by, where sports of various kinds had been organized, and were well carried out under the superintendence of Mr. Middleton and other gentlemen. As the daylight began to wane, we all returned to the barn, where we were entertained by music, songs and recitations in a most agreeable manner. The evening's proceedings closed by Mr. Hedderly proposing the health of Her Majesty, a proposition which was most heartily welcomed and loyally received.

At Burton Joyce

the National School Room was soon made gay with various flags, conspicuous among them being Royal Standards and Union Jacks. The Congregational School Room was tastefully and profusely festooned with flowers. A line of flags floated across the main street and others were hung out from houses nearby. Festoons of evergreens and Chinese lanterns marked the entrance to Mr Cordon's grounds, which had kindly been placed at the disposal of the Sports Sub-committee.

A procession was formed at 1.30 p.m. and marched up to the railway station to meet the band. Preceded by their lively music, the procession then went to the end of the village and returned to the schools.

At 4.00 p.m., and again at 5.00 p.m., tables were laid in each schoolroom. During the afternoon about seven hundred of our parishioners enjoyed an excellent meal and one another's company at these tables.

The vicar felt it was a great pleasure to have sitting next to him an old veteran who well remembered the Jubilee of 1809. Quarter-master Sergeant Swinscoe was then a farm lad working on the Hill Farm, at present occupied by Mr Cheshire. He now wears a medal gained in the first Burmese War when serving his country in the old Nottinghamshire 45th (or Sherwood Foresters) Regiment, and for the last forty-nine years he has enjoyed a well-merited Staff-Sergeant's pension.

Before separating, the vicar begged the company, one and all, to let the Union Jacks that surrounded them be typical of the union of feeling and unity of purpose that should animate all Englishmen. He remarked that even bad systems of government have occasionally been administered by good rules, while good systems of government have, unfortunately, sometimes had bad heads; but he claimed with thankfulness that those in England were blessed with both a good system of government and a right good head of it in the person of Her Majesty Queen Victoria. Feeling sure that all would agree with him in holding that opinion, he called for three hearty cheers for the queen, which were given with the enthusiasm of a loyal people.

The sports afterwards were remarkable and, we had almost said, unexpectedly good. Indeed there had never been any so well ordered and so well contested in Burton Joyce. The prizes gained by the fortunate winners were both many and elegant.

The year 1893 was marked by the wedding of Queen Victoria's grandson, Prince George (later King George V), to Princess Mary of Teck. Once again the parish magazine described the day's events:

The Royal Wedding Day was loyally kept in both our parishes. In Bulcote a very successful gathering was arranged for all the children of the village. After a good tea, races were arranged and prizes and medals were distributed.

At Burton Joyce Mr. Brett kindly lent his field and many of the parishioners helped in various ways. As so many festivities took place on the same day all our friends could not be present, as some were at the Bulcote tea and others at the Tennis Club gathering.

The Drum and Fife Band, conducted by Mr. Sansome, met the children at the school, marched with them down to the field and played nearly all the evening. A most bountiful picnic tea had been provided; indeed some of the helpers were rather doubtful whether all the buns could possibly be eaten, but the very last vanished and the children were then ready for handfuls of sweets which seemed literally to rain down as in the good old times of fairy tales. Races were then organized, and the winners received orders on Mr. Beecroft's well-known shop. Nuts and biscuits were then scrambled for, and the merry party broke up after listening to the National Anthem from the Band and joining heartily in the three cheers proposed by the Vicar for our Queen and all the Royal Family, as well as for our Burton Joyce friends who had planned this pleasant day. The proverbial 'Queen's weather' helped to make the gathering in every way a success, and encouraged many parents and elder brothers and sisters to join the children during the evening. A medal in memory of the day has since been given to each schoolchild.

A poster for the 1953 coronation festivities in Burton Joyce

A coronation party at Bulcote Farm, 1953

Some sixty years later the coronation of Queen Elizabeth II was celebrated in the villages with a week-long programme of activities, described in multicoloured posters. These included village hall Coronation Capers and children's sports. Similarly in Bulcote, funds were raised by a series of dances, whist drives, concerts, etc. in order to entertain some two hundred people to a meal in 'the big granary at Bulcote' on Coronation Day.

CHAPTER SEVEN

Notable People

WINIFRED BLAGG

Winifred Blagg came to live at The Hall, Burton Joyce, with her father, Henry, and mother, Agnes, in 1890, when she was eleven years old. She was the youngest of five children. The family soon entered into the life of the village, giving generously to the various appeals for money such as the school, church restorations (St Helen's and Holy Trinity), the Flower Show and Carnarvon Reading Room. In 1894 the magazine records that 'A handsome silver Chalice and Paten were presented to our Church of St Helen, on Sunday 12 August, by Mr and Mrs Blagg, of The Hall, as a thank-offering on completing the 25th year of their married life.' Henry and his sons, Harry and Tom, were also keen members of the Cricket Club for many

Miss Winifred Blagg (far right) at the wartime wedding of her nephew, Guy Allen, to Joan Wright. Guy was chairman of Bulcote Parish Council from 1973 to 1990

The drawing-room, Burton Joyce Hall

years, eventually becoming vice-presidents. In 1908 the family left The Hall to go and live in the new semi-detached house on Willow Wong known as Willow Way.

A very intelligent girl, Winifred left home to get her degree, and for a while was the headmistress of a girls' school in Bristol until recalled home by her father to take charge of the running of the house. This must have been very frustrating for a girl of her abilities but, characteristically, instead of bewailing her lot, she used her gift for organization by entering fully into county and village affairs. One of the first things she did was to found the Hockey Club in 1919, and after four years of hard work the members began to feel they had a team 'somewhat worthy of the name'. In May 1894 she had been confirmed into the church and was to be a devout member of St Helen's all her life, serving on the Parochial Church Council, organizing fund-raising events and running the Girls' Friendly Society. One such fund-raising effort concerned the central heating for the church in 1955. She said in an interview that

the new gas heating plant had ended a legend that used to frighten the village children. When the church was heated by a boiler, the clerk used to nip downstairs during the sermon to stoke it. Loud rumbling noises would echo round the church through an iron grating in the floor – and wide-eyed youngsters would whisper to one another 'It's hell down there.'

Winifred is remembered for two things in particular: first for the founding of the Burton Joyce and Bulcote Branch of the Women's Institute, and second for her indefatigable work in raising money for the village hall. Her life was succinctly summed up by J.P.H. Bratley in the parish magazine after her death in 1961:

Winifred May Blagg – an Appreciation
'You know Miss Blagg then.' This was often said to me on meeting people in the County for the first time, when they learned that I lived in Burton Joyce.

The explanation was not far to seek. Miss Blagg's work and influence in the field of women's activities spread far beyond the confines of Burton Joyce and profoundly affected the development of those two important organizations, the Women's Institute and the Nursing Association throughout the county. For these movements she had an untiring zeal and brought to both great gifts of inspiration and far-sightedness. The Burton Joyce branch of the former became, under her

The Village Hall Committee, *c.* 1928. Miss Blagg is seated

Presidency for nearly 25 years, one of the strongest and most virile in Nottinghamshire. When the County Council took over the responsibility for a comprehensive nursing service she played a large part in the initial stages and for many years was a co-opted member of the County Welfare Committee. But these wider activities were simply an over-flow from her main interests which centred in the Village and people of Burton Joyce. In all Parish life, particularly in that of the Church, she took a leading share and supplemented her strenuous efforts with large and timely giving. Everything in the village was her personal concern and she possessed an amazing knowledge of its people and their doings . . . Allied to her unfailing enthusiasm was clear thinking and sound judgement, together with frankness and out-spokenness. If at times the latter was somewhat provocative her experience and wisdom never failed to command respect. The driving force behind this dynamic personality was a deep religious faith, unclouded by doubt and the fruits of this faith found expression, not in vague benevolence, but in positive and practice service. She would have scorned the term 'duty'. Hers was a complete and joyous offering of herself in the service of her fellows.

Three months before she died Winifred went into a nursing home, knowing her days were numbered and facing up to this realization with characteristic calmness and courage. She wrote a farewell letter to the magazine in October 1960. In it she said:

As I have been a member of St. Helen's for the last 70 years, having come to the village as a little girl of eleven, I have naturally known many people; it pleases me much to learn that Mrs. Williams [the Vicar's wife] and family are going to occupy our old family pew, which went with the Hall, where we lived for eighteen years. I am very happily settled at the Convent Nursing Home where I hope to stay till I get my call. I feel rather like Christian who rested in the land of the Delectable Mountains till he forded the river. I have been much helped by the prayers of my friends in bringing me to this happy state of quiet waiting . . . Please don't grieve at my departure. I have had, in many ways, a long and satisfying life; and I wish my last service to be one of thankfulness for this.

JOHN AND EDWARD PEART BRETT

It was in 1759 that the Brett family first appeared in the parish registers with the marriage of William Brett of Lowdham to Mary Park of Burton Joyce. William occupied a farm belonging to the Earl of Chesterfield on Lambley

John Brett in the uniform of the South Nottinghamshire Yeomanry

An advertisement for Brett Brothers City Brewery

Lane, on the site of Nos 22, 24 and 26. Later they moved down the road to the farm at No. 2, today known as Beaconsfield House. John and Edward were the great-grandsons of William and Mary. John, who was born in 1822, joined the South Nottinghamshire Hussars Yeomanry (a part-time organization similar to the Territorial Army) when he was seventeen and became a sergeant-major. He was also a farmer at Lowdham. It was another brother, Frederick William, who succeeded to Brett's Farm as it became known. John's farming career ended when his herd was struck with the dreaded foot-and-mouth disease, which left him in financial difficulties, for in those days there was no compensation. He left for York to join his brother Edward Peart, who had made a success in the brewing industry, and died there in 1898.

Edward, who was born in 1826, never forgot his roots and always took an interest in his native village. A pen-portrait of him appeared in *The York Magazine* of 1885. It describes him as the 'head of the well-known firm of Messrs. Brett Brothers, wine and spirit merchants, City Brewery, York'. It also mentions that he was educated in Nottingham at the Standard Hill Academy, and that in his young days, before he left for York, 'he took a lively interest in agricultural matters and was one of the first to introduce the steam threshing machine into the district'. The article concludes by saying that 'Mr. Brett has worked his way up from a small beginning, and his present position is sufficient guarantee that honest work, untiring energy, and sound principles are certain in the long run, to meet with their just recompense.' Edward's daughter Mia married Tom Terry, the son of Sir Joseph Terry, the chocolate magnate of York.

Edward was one of the first subscribers for the stained glass in the east window of St Helen's church. In the parish magazine of May 1887 the vicar wrote:

> To shew how well the scheme for our East Window is now being received in parts even removed from Burton Joyce, we may mention that by much the greater number of the foregoing sums have been subscribed by those who live far away from us; and it is with the greatest satisfaction that the Vicar is able to announce that he received a most genial and generous letter from Mr. Edward Brett, of York on the subject. This gentleman, not content with being the first to put down his name for £5.5s.0d. in 1885, writes that he now means to canvass his friends at home and abroad, with a result that he feels sure will be satisfactory to those who lived in his much respected native village. May his example of generosity and zeal be widely followed by others!

In the June 1888 edition of the magazine the vicar announces that the window is to be put in the following month and also that Mr. Brett of York 'has most generously promised to increase his original subscription to a quarter of the total sum needed, which is estimated to be about £130'.

In 1902 Edward purchased Brett's Farm. His brother continued to live there until ill-health forced him to leave. It was then sold, in 1908, to J.C. Woodsend.

ELIJAH LINLEY

> There died on Saturday night at Burton Joyce, one of the eldest residents in the person of Mr. Elijah Linley, who was born on 30 July 1824, thus being in his 90th year. For over 60 years he had held the office of parish clerk, having been appointed on August 4th, 1844. The deceased was a framework knitter working for many years at his own frame. He was born in the same cottage in which he died. He had lived in the reign of five Sovereigns and had tolled the bell for four.

So ran the *Nottingham Guardian* obituary of Elijah Linley on 17 November 1913, summing up very well the life of this unusual man.

Elijah's grandfather first came to Burton Joyce in the late eighteenth

Elijah Linley outside the north door of St Helen's
church when he was eighty-five

century and founded a prolific family. His second son had ten children, and in
the following generation families of ten and eleven were not unusual. Most of
Elijah's family had the sort of names common at the time – William, John,
Robert – so one wonders why his father chose to name his last three sons
Elijah, Elisha and Titus. Elijah outlived all of his siblings by over half a
century, the last dying in 1853.

The cottage where Elijah was born, lived and died no longer exists, having
been pulled down in the 1960s to make way for the present Langham Drive.
It stood on the north side of Main Street about halfway from the centre of the
village towards Bulcote, backing on to the hillside and, in his early years,
facing open farmland.

Little is known of the family's background, but they were probably a little
better off than some of their neighbours: the cottage looks comparatively
substantial, and Elijah must have had some education to be able to take on the
job of parish clerk at the age of twenty. With ten children to bring up in a
period when very little education was available to the poor, and none was
free, this was quite an achievement for his father who, like his son, was parish
clerk and a framework knitter. Elijah's father died in 1844 at the age of fifty-
seven.

The appointment of the parish clerk was in the hands of the vicar, who
from 1822 to 1863 was John Rolleston, so he presumably approved the

Elijah Linley's cottage, Main Street

succession of Elijah to his father's position. He would then have been licensed, probably by the archdeacon. The work of the parish clerk varied in different parishes and at different periods – in earlier times it was quite usual for him to be someone in holy orders unable to find a living. However, by the nineteenth century this was no longer common and the work of the parish clerk was to arrange baptisms, communions, weddings and burials, and to keep the registers. He also acted as sexton, ringing the bells and sometimes even leading the responses, and digging the graves.

Elijah was also the verger, so he had to clean the church, wash the surplices, stoke the boiler and maintain the churchyard. It is stated that he dug 1,100 graves and attended 400 marriages and 1,500 baptisms! He is reputed to have been very agile in his younger days: the church then had three bells and he managed to ring all three, jumping about on the steps of the font, which at that time stood under the tower.

Between 1885 and 1895 the parish magazine published the church accounts. These show that Elijah was paid £13 a year as parish clerk, and that in 1889 he also received £2 for cleaning the church, £2 3s. 6d. for the churchyard and £2 12s. 6d. for washing surplices. In addition he received a small fee for each wedding, baptism and burial, as well as payment for digging graves.

Since he was his own master, Elijah's second occupation of framework knitter would have fitted in easily. Unlike many of the knitters Elijah apparently owned his frame, so would have been free to work as much or as little as he chose. No doubt he worked as much as possible, as he is described as being a thrifty man and soon had a family to maintain. He married Mary Shelton from Carlton in April 1847, when he was twenty-five and she was twenty-four. They enjoyed a long married life together until her death in 1902. Their six children, four boys and two girls, all attended school, by now presumably the local National School. Most of them worked in some aspect of framework knitting as they grew older, but in 1875 the younger daughter, Mary, known as Polly or more commonly Polly'lijah, became a monitress in the school at the age of thirteen. She progressed to become pupil teacher when her indentures were signed in 1879, then finally became a certificated teacher in 1884, remaining for many years at the local school. The school inspectors found her efficient, but some parents complained about her harsh treatment of the infants.

Elijah was apparently sufficiently thrifty to maintain his family and save enough money to buy the cottage in which he was born and lived. He was not miserly, however, as he subscribed to good causes, for example giving 10s. for church repairs in 1895. As parish clerk he must have given satisfaction, for in the magazine for March 1894 we read of a presentation to him for long service:

Elijah Linley and his wife, Mary

On February 4th Elijah Linley completed his 50th year of service as Parish Clerk, and in honour of the occasion a presentation was made to him in token of the kindly feelings of his fellow parishioners. Mrs. Goodall was kind enough to undertake the collections, and on Feb. 3rd, the Vicar in the presence of the Churchwardens, Sidesmen and Mrs. Goodall, presented Elijah Linley with a purse containing £22.5s., together with a parchment bearing the names of the subscribers to the number of about eighty. Elijah Linley was much gratified at such a kind expression of goodwill and specially desired to offer his most heartfelt thanks to all the subscribers through the medium of the Parish Magazine.

Elijah was a member of the Odd Fellows (the Albion Glory Lodge founded in 1833), which met at The Cross Keys monthly. It was basically a Friendly Society providing free medical care, sick pay and a funeral grant in return for a regular subscription. In 1877 Elijah appears to have been the senior member of the lodge. He may have needed this insurance as he grew older. In the Easter vestry minutes for 1907 it was

unanimously agreed that the Vicar write a letter of sympathy to Mr Elijah Linley in his illness and also to express the grateful recognition of his faithful service for upward of 68 years as Parish Clerk and Sexton. Mr Fortescue announced that a subscription list had been started with the object of creating a small pension for Mr. Linley, and which he hoped would be heartily supported.

In spite of his increasing infirmity, Elijah continued to hold the appointment until his death, although for a number of years he was not able to undertake the more active jobs. Perhaps his son did these for him, but he apparently still worked his knitting frame and pottered in his garden. In his obituary in the *Nottingham Evening News* it was said that

his memories of things which had happened in his younger days were remarkably interesting, and he used to talk very pleasantly of the various vicars under whom he had served (five altogether) . . . . Although not a great traveller, he was one of the earliest passengers on the opening of the Midland line from Nottingham to Lincoln.

After an illness of only a few days, Elijah died at the age of eighty-nine and was buried at Burton Joyce on 15 November 1913.

HARRY WEBSTER ROBERTS

The Roberts family came to live in Burton Joyce in 1875. By the time of the 1881 census Henry Roberts, a silk agent from Nottingham, was a widower of seventy. In the same household lived his daughter Caroline, who was presumably in charge of the household, Ellen Louise, a dressmaker, Bertha, a musician and professor of music, and Henry (Harry) Webster, also a silk agent, aged thirty at this time. The rest of Henry junior's life was to be spent in this village, involved in its activities, into which he entered whole-heartedly. He married Sophia Alvey, a Burton Joyce girl, daughter of Joseph and Ann Alvey.

Harry was a man for 'getting things done' and probably did more to change the face of Burton Joyce than any other single person, before or since. He was the driving force behind the local Co-operative Building Society (see Chapter 2). Indeed, one of the first houses to be built on Criftin Road was his own home, Fernside. He was a pillar of the local Methodist church, where he was superintendent of the Sunday School from 1879 to 1924 and treasurer on the committee that built the new church in 1908.

In 1926 the Roberts family left the village to go to live in Ulverston, and an illuminated address was presented to them in commemoration of their half

Harry Webster Roberts

The Roberts Recreation Ground

century's residence in Burton Joyce. All old friends, besides the Wesleyans, were invited to sign. They did not forget their church, however. In 1931 the Methodist church had electric light installed and was generally renovated throughout. The cost of the work, so the parish magazine related,

> has been the generous gift of Mr. H.W. Roberts, who wrote expressing his and Mrs. Roberts' desire to do something for the Church, to mark the Jubilee of their wedding, and also in memory of the many happy years of Christian fellowship, spent in connection with that Church, when they lived at Burton Joyce.

What Harry is most remembered for, however, is his donation of land to the village for the recreation ground, still known today as the Roberts Recreation Ground. On 23 May 1925 it was opened with much pomp and ceremony by Mrs Roberts. The parish council was there in force, led by the chairman, Mr J.G. Short. Other dignitaries included the vicar, the Revd C.T. Witherington, who gave the prayers of dedication, Mr D.E. Gale, clerk to the council, and Messrs Massey, Woodsend, Hearnshaw, Blagg, Cullen, Poole and

Cragg, etc. A report of the occasion was given in *The Trader and Citizen* on 6 June. After she had unlocked the gates Mrs Roberts handed over the key to the chairman of the parish council.

> the doors were opened, and the crowd of villagers headed by the members of the parish council and the donors, walked in procession by the north walk to the small pavilion that has been erected and looks quite picturesque with its belt of trees and the parish church in the near background. It was here that the main programme of dedication was gone through, the proceedings being opened by the singing of 'All things bright and beautiful' by the United Church and Wesleyan choirs.

The highlight of the afternoon was the speech by Harry Roberts, in which he gave a detailed account of his life in Burton Joyce. This is of so much interest that it is included here, almost in full:

Mr. Roberts' interesting Reminiscences
This is a jubilee to me: within two or three weeks I shall have lived in your midst 50 years. I came here at the end of June, 1875, and I think I am celebrating my jubilee in as good a way as I possibly could. [Applause] I have never regretted coming to Burton Joyce: my life here has been very happy. It would have been impossible – I realise it now; I did not then – for me to have a more beautiful village in which to reside. [Hear, hear] I look upon Burton Joyce as being in the very forefront of all the villages of our county of Nottinghamshire.

We have that magnificent hill on the north, and the very beautiful river on the other side of our village. We have, too, a very fine body of people, young and old and of all kinds, living amongst us. But I have another reason for being glad that I came to live at Burton Joyce, and that is that I found my wife here. Of course you will expect me to say that while I am thankful for many things, I am most thankful for the great gift that came into my life then many years ago. You have been very kind to me at Burton Joyce during those fifty years. No one knows better than I do – I think the Chairman meant to allude to it just now – that I have been somewhat troublesome. [Laughter] We have had our ups and downs in Burton Joyce in those fifty years, but I think I would like to promise you one thing, that whatever the past has been – and you may reckon it up as you like – I shall not give you the same amount of trouble during the next fifty years. [Laughter] Now I have been looking back at the happenings of the last fifty years. This village is not the same today. There are many changes here, and I would like to say it very heartily and for the good of everyone, that the changes that have taken place in fifty years in Burton Joyce are changes for the better. [Hear, hear] You would not vote to go back to the state of things that existed here half a century ago. We have our regrets, and I hope you have. First of all – and the older ones will understand when I say it – I regret very much that there is not a cricket club in Burton Joyce. During the early part of my life here we had a cricket club, and it was one of my special joys to take part in the cricket life amongst you. We had men living at Burton Joyce who could play cricket, and though Nottingham was celebrated for its cricket then, we had two players in this village who were nearly as good as any two men in the county. One was Tom Cragg, who lives amongst you today, and the other Jack Cartledge. I have known each of them many a time to take five wickets. They were splendid bowlers; we never had, and I think we never shall have, two such cricketers as they were. Then I have another regret, and so have you. We have lost the music of the handframe knitter's machine. One of the pleasures of a walk in the streets of the village was here and there to hear the whirr of the frame – 'pepper and salt', as they used to call it. These days will never come again, but I think they will never be forgotten. But I am going to mention two other things – the names of two persons. If I have any vivid remembrance of any two people in Burton Joyce it is of these. Many of you who never knew them will be surprised. One was the old postmistress – Pattie Jackson. She was a charming woman. She handed you a tray of stamps and you helped yourself. [Laughter] There was always the utmost confidence in Pattie's mind that everybody to whom the tray was presented would pay for what they took. Perhaps that would not happen today. There was another lady: and ladies of those days were different to the ladies of today. [Laughter] She was a fine lady, especially when she was dressed in her silk or satin – I forget which – and that was old Mrs. Harby. And even in those olden times there were some gentlemen who were connected with Basford Council, such as Fred and William Brett, Mark Baguley and Joseph Alvey. Those names are associated with Basford, just as our friend Mr. Short's is today . . . We have a Parish Council. Fifty years ago we had a vestry meeting: and we knew what was taking place there. We used to have the schoolroom crowded and many times there was something to enjoy. [Laughter] Once we had a very difficult business in hand I remember – the lighting of the streets of Burton Joyce. That was a tremendous time, and it was one of the great pleasures of my life. We held three meetings in the National School in successive weeks. On the first two nights we could not come to a decision, but on the third

The old post office (behind the lamp) of Pattie Jackson's time

night we agreed that we would have lights, for the simple reason that somebody made me stand up and talk away until everybody was tired [Laughter] – so they went home and we passed the resolution and got the lights. [Renewed laughter] Nobody today would ever think of not having the streets of Burton Joyce lighted, but in those days there were people who did. Then, again, I can remember the growth of the village. During the last fifty years I reckon there have been 202 new houses built in Burton Joyce. Most of those were due to the Building Society which was started in 1881. During the career of that Society we bought something like 28 acres of land – four, five or six lots – which was sold again for £7,000. That was the means of a very considerable extension of the village which we have today in Criftin Road, Wellington Road, Shaftesbury Avenue, Gordon Road and St. Helen's Grove. We sold some 6,000 yards of land at a shilling a yard with free conveyance and the roads made and paid for. You are not able to do that today. And so we have seen the progress that has been made in our Village. It is much better than it was fifty years ago, and I am going to make a prophecy, viz: that I believe within the next twenty or thirty years this village will be much better than it is today. Now Mrs. Roberts and I are looking forward to living a little while longer. You have borne with me a long time this afternoon, but I want to say a word to the young people. I love young people. Ever since I came to Burton Joyce I have taught in the Sunday School and sought to help and guide the young people of this village. Boys and girls and young people, you have here a goodly heritage in this piece of land that has been given to you. There never was more done for young people than is being done today. I know that parents in the olden times were good, but you boys and girls have better food, better clothes and better homes than most of the children of fifty years ago had. There has been a great improvement in these matters; I have enjoyed seeing it, and I feel certain it will continue. This recreation ground is intended to help you to be strong and healthy. My last word is this: let every boy and girl make the best use of this ground day by day and week by week while you are young. See that it is used for the purpose for which it is intended, and it will make you happier perhaps than you otherwise would have been.

The account of the proceedings then continued:

After the ceremony Mr. and Mrs. Roberts entertained all the children of the village to tea in the parish school, and the members of the parish council, a number of personal friends and the choirs in the Wesleyan school-room. Presents of sweets were made to the children by whom, perhaps more than anyone, this will be looked back upon as a great and memorable day. After tea in the Wesleyan schoolroom Mr. Mozley initiated, and Mr. Blagg supported, a very hearty vote of thanks to Mr. and Mrs. Roberts for their hospitality. The united choirs of the parish church and the Wesleyan church were conducted by Mr. J. Lees, choirmaster of the latter, and Mr. Stewart, organist of the parish church, officiated at the harmonium.

When the bypass was cut through the village in 1930/1, a substantial part of the ground was requisitioned by the county council. As the parish magazine of April 1933 related, the money received from this purchase was spent on refurbishing the ground by the parish council:

This beautiful playground for the young children of the village has been thoroughly renovated, levelled, and in other ways adapted for its purpose. The wall which forms the boundary on the Chestnut Grove side has been repaired, and new iron fencing has been fixed where required; also the fencing on the by-pass road has been raised in part so as to make it more uniform. The shelter which was in a broken-down condition has also been efficiently restored. Added to all this, a supply of playground equipment, consisting of a slide, merry-go-round, three swings and a jolly rocking horse have been provided, so that the youngsters may have plenty of exercise and thoroughly enjoy themselves when they visit the ground.

Certainly Mr Roberts' last words, 'let every boy and girl make the best use of this ground day by day and week by week', have been fulfilled. Thousands of local children have benefited from his generosity. There have been changes. Over the years equipment has been replaced and brought up to date. In recent years more equipment, to suit all ages, has been added with special safety surfaces. An enclosed area for ball games is a further attraction, and in 1993 a splendid new helter-skelter slide was installed. Mr Roberts would have approved.

JOSEPH SANSOME

Joseph Sansome was schoolmaster of Burton Joyce National School from 1878 to 1914, coming to the school at about the time when education was being made compulsory. His appointment showed a determination on the

Joseph Sansome

The old school building, where Joseph Sansome taught, *c.* 1950

part of the school managers to improve the standard of education in the village. The school was one of the National Schools run under the aegis of the Church of England, and owed its establishment to voluntary subscriptions. The building (now referred to as the Old School) of which Joseph was appointed master was the second school to be built, on land given by the Earl of Chesterfield with money raised mainly by subscription (the earl gave £100) and a small grant from the National Society. It was opened in January 1868. A very small government grant was available, and since 1862 this had been administered on the 'Payment by Results' system, which means that government inspectors descended on the school annually to examine the children, and on their report the grant was based.

The previous schoolmistress, Miss Parrott, had struggled to improve the school without qualified assistance, and short of money and equipment. Apparently the managers felt dissatisfied, and at a meeting in July 1878 asked the vicar, who was the chairman, to 'make enquiries with reference to an efficient schoolmaster'. At the next meeting the Revd A.G. Munro Meugens read a letter he had received recommending Mr J. Sansome of Newcastle, Staffordshire, who was promptly invited for interview with the vicar and the treasurer, Mr Snooke, from The Hall. After hearing an account of the interview and the candidate's testimonials, the managers appointed Joseph to the mastership at an annual salary of £100, 'it being understood that for that sum he will act as organist at Burton Joyce and Bulcote Church and help with the Sunday School as required'.

Joseph, who was born in Coventry, the son of John Sansome, a gardener, was at this time an unmarried man of twenty-three. He was a certificated teacher, and this may have been his second post, following his time in Newcastle-under-Lyme. He settled down for thirty-six years in Burton Joyce. At first he found lodgings with the family of George Stanton, a retired lace manufacturer living at Prospect House, Mount Pleasant, at the very top of Willow Wong, now called 'The Mount'. He shared the home with Stanton and his wife, both aged seventy-nine, their two unmarried daughters, and a woman lodger and her daughter.

Nine years later Joseph married Charlotte Mary Whitchurch of Gedling, eleven years his junior, and they moved into a house in the newly developed area of Wellington Road. In July 1887 he sent the following letter to the parish magazine:

To the Parishioners of Burton Joyce and Bulcote.

My dear Friends,

It has given me very great pleasure to accept from the Vicar, on your behalf, the very handsome testimonial presented to me on the morning of my marriage, June 2nd, and also the good wishes of all, so kindly expressed by the Rev. R.W. Thompson, on that occasion, both for my wife and myself. Had anything been wanting to complete our happiness, it would have been supplied by your kind wishes for our welfare.

During the nine years I have resided among you, I have ever received kindness from all with whom I have come in contact, not only in connection with school affairs, but in whatever position I may have been placed, and it gives my wife and myself much pleasure to know that at the commencement of our married life we still possess your good wishes, and I trust we may deserve them better in the future than I have done in the past.

Again thanking you heartily,

Believe me, yours faithfully,

JOSEPH SANSOME.

The 1891 census records that at this time his widowed mother-in-law was living with them (on her own means) and that they had two children: a son, Sidney, aged three, and a daughter, Elsie Margaret, only four months old. They employed a seventeen-year-old girl as a general domestic servant.

Joseph seems to have been conscientious and hard-working, and set about building up the school. The average attendance gradually increased, which made it easier to improve the standard of work, and after a few years the inspectors' reports became complimentary. On the occasion of Joseph's marriage the vicar wrote:

Mr. Sansome's worth and work are too well known and valued to need any remarks here farther than the statement that between forty and fifty of our parishioners gladly seized the occasion of his marriage to present him with a testimonial which they could have wished had been more worthy of his acceptance. During his nine years of office here he has been a good friend to all of us, to none more than to the Vicar and his family. Our well-filled Church, when he was married, witness to the interest taken in his future by all classes amongst us, and the children of the schools proved how they respected him by presenting him with an elegant centre-piece for flowers.

Even allowing for the usual hyperbole common on such occasions, it is plain that Joseph was much respected. In March 1895 the vicar again noted in the magazine:

NATIONAL SCHOOL.
The Managers have the greatest pleasure in referring to the report of H.M. Inspector.
   The nature of that report is shown in the fact that the highest possible Government Grant has been earned by the School in the past year. This could not have been done but for the interest and intelligence which Mr. Sansome and the Assistant Teachers have brought to bear upon their work.

This was endorsed by an article about the village in the *Weekly Express* for 9 September 1895:

Considering the population, an average attendance of 150 at the school may be deemed good evidence as to the manner in which it fulfils the requirements of the place, and if confirmation were wanted it is to be found in the fact that last year an 'excellent' grant was obtained as a result of the annual inspection.

The grant in question was for £125 8s. 6d. It had increased consistently from 1884, the earliest date in the minute book, when it was only £46. 2s. 10d. In these days of inflation we tend to assume that such an increase is normal, but Joseph's salary rose only slowly from £100 to £120 in 1881, and by £10 instalments to £150 in 1902.
   Joseph was expected to work hard. The only holidays for the school at first were occasional days: it was only in the 1890s that the present system of three terms became established, with short breaks at Christmas and Easter and a

Joseph Sansome with his class

fortnight in August. This latter holiday was extended to a month in 1903. In addition to Joseph there was a qualified assistant to teach the infants in a separate room, and at least one pupil teacher, but until 1893 they had to work in the same room, separated by only a curtain. In 1893 a partition was installed at the suggestion of the inspectors at a cost of £19. This must have been a great help, for with numbers approaching 150, of whom just under a third were infants, there would have been about 100 children in the big room.

Joseph was obviously a sincerely religious man, for the inspectors commented especially on the very high standard of scripture teaching in the school. In 1889 Canon Were, who had started a young men's bible class in the village, was made Bishop of Derby. The vicar was keen for the class to continue, and was delighted when Joseph volunteered for the job, commenting that 'no-one could possibly be more acceptable', and since the class continued to prosper the young men evidently shared his opinion. It must have made Joseph's Sundays busy, as they met at 2.30 p.m. every Sunday except for the first in the month, and he already had to play the organ for three services.

Though playing the organ was required of him, Joseph seems to have been interested in music in any case. He taught singing in the school and from time to time concerts were organized, usually for fund-raising purposes, when the children sang quite difficult works. In January 1888, for example, the vicar wrote in the magazine: 'On the 16th, we had a very pleasing performance of a Cantata "The Indian Summer" by the School Children. Competent judges of singing give Mr Sansome the utmost credit for training the children so well as he has.' This particular concert raised money to award prizes for good attendance at school, so no doubt all concerned had a personal interest! As a result thirty children were awarded prizes.

In 1891 Sergeant Pounder started a drum and fife band. It was most successful and ran a competition for individual players in September, while on Christmas Day, according to the vicar, the band marched round the parish playing 'pretty pieces'. However, when the band played in July 1893 for the Royal Wedding celebrations, we read that: 'The Drum and Fife Band,

The illuminated address presented to Joseph Sansome on his retirement in 1914

conducted by Mr Sansome, met the children at the school, marched with them down to the field (where races and a picnic tea were organised) and played nearly all the evening.'

Joseph had become a valuable and respected member of the local community. His own family prospered: his son won a Nottinghamshire County Council Scholarship and his daughter a scholarship to Nottingham Girls' High School. A few older inhabitants of the village can just remember being at school under his care in the last few years before the First World War, and their impression is of a strict but much respected man.

Joseph finally left Burton Joyce in March 1914, at the age of fifty-nine, when the whole family emigrated to Canada. A 'testimonial fund' was organized and Miss Maud Thompson, daughter of the former vicar, wrote in a letter: 'Indeed he has deserved well of the whole village and we personally owe him a great debt of gratitude.'

J.H. SCOTT

John Henry Scott was born in the parish of St Mary in the Sherwood district of Nottingham on 27 July 1865. His father, Henry, was a master carpenter and builder, with a successful building business that he carried on at premises

John Henry Scott

A wedding photograph of John Henry
Scott and his bride

in Chaucer Street, Great Freeman Street and on Leenside. Henry came to
Nottingham from Cambridge having heard of the opportunities for good
builders. The family lived on Matlock Street and later Sherwood Street in
Nottingham, where John Henry was born.

Records in his cash-book show that Henry rented the Chaucer Street
premises in February 1893, paying a quarterly rent of £4 3s. 4d. In January
1893 his Leenside shop cost him £2 10s. 6d. in rent. In 1893 he rented
premises in Burton Joyce where he came to live at No. 10 Main Street, for
which on 25 March of that year he paid £4 10s. 0d. A later entry shows that
on 1 July 1893 he paid a quarterly rent of £6 5s. 0d. The family lived in these
premises while their new house, Bulcote Mount, was being built. Henry
bought the land in Bulcote for £500, the agreement stating that he had to
'build one or a pair of houses to the value of £1500'. His family moved into
their new house in the mid-1890s. *Kelly's Directory* of 1900 shows Henry
Scott as a builder in Burton Joyce and a resident at Bulcote Mount.

John Henry was only partially trained in the building business, which he
eventually took over from his father early in 1893. Owing to his lack of
expertise and interest this once flourishing business gradually declined. He
was much more interested in travelling and photography. His travels took him

Bulcote Mount in winter, *c.* 1900

to Guernsey and to Ireland, where it is thought he met his future wife at Malin Head. They were married on 18 June 1900, when John Henry was thirty-six, and they had six children.

His interest in photography led John Henry to explore his local area, travelling in a pony and trap taking photographs as he went through Lowdham, Gunthorpe, Hoveringham, Gonalston, Epperstone, Rolleston, Fiskerton, Morton and Averham. He was particularly interested in the churches and did much wedding photography. However, most of his work was confined to Burton Joyce and Bulcote, where he recorded all of the main buildings and activities over a period of many years until his death in 1946. John Henry did his own developing and printing.

In 1904 *Kelly's Directory* lists John Henry, in Bulcote, as assistant overseer, which involved him in the business of collecting rates, etc. When the war came he was employed on 'war work' at Chilwell Ordnance Factory and also at Lawrence's, the furniture manufacturers. In 1925 he became clerk to Gunthorpe Parish Council. He also compiled the electoral rolls for the parishes of Bulcote, Lowdham, Gunthorpe, Epperstone, Oxton and Gonalston.

It is, however, his photography for which John Henry will be most remembered. His photographs stand as a vivid memory of life in the villages of the Trent Valley, particularly Burton Joyce and Bulcote, in the early twentieth century, and provide a fitting epitaph. Many of his photographs appear in this book.

THE REVD REGINALD W. THOMPSON

The Revd Reginald Ward Thompson became vicar of Burton Joyce with Bulcote in 1884 in succession to the Revd Allan George Munro Meugens, who moved to Carlton at the time of the building and opening of St Paul's church. Reginald was about fifty-six when he came to the village, his family consisting of his wife (two years younger), his two daughters, Edith Elizabeth (twenty-six) and Maud Mary (twenty-four), and his son, Reginald Beviss (twenty-one). There was also another son, Geoffrey Reginald, who became a doctor. He must have been older and left home before 1884. Reginald was born in London, son of Francis Thompson, but we have no knowledge of his earlier career as he came late to the ministry of the Church. He had an Oxford MA but was forty-five when he matriculated in 1873. He was made a

The Revd Reginald Ward
Thompson, vicar of Burton Joyce

Mrs Thompson and her daughter Maud Mary

deacon in 1877 and a priest in 1878. His first post was as curate at St Stephen's, Westminster, where he was remembered with affection, and his wife and daughters were much involved in parish work as they were later in Burton Joyce. The 1891 census tells us that he employed a cook, a housemaid and a garden boy. They lived in the old vicarage in Vicarage Drive, which was then comparatively new and must have had a very pleasant outlook over open fields.

By 1904, when he left the village to retire to Rugby, Reginald was seventy-six. Indeed, he described himself in December 1893 on the occasion of a dinner for the 'old folks' as one of the old folks himself, and this is how he appears in photographs of the time: a white-haired, bewhiskered, dignified old gentleman.

Reginald's most lasting gift to the village has proved to be the starting of the parish magazine, which he began in January 1895, soon after his arrival, and which at first he wrote entirely himself. It is from his regular letters and his choice of topics that we can learn something of his life, work, beliefs and character during the first ten years of his ministry, from which we are fortunate enough to have copies of the magazine. We read of his personal happiness and tragedies in its pages. The year after he came, on Christmas Eve, his elder daughter was taken ill and died of pneumonia after a short illness. In his January letter he refers to his sorrow and thanks his parishioners for their prayers and help. In February there was a tribute from the parish magazine of St Stephen's, Westminster. A happier occasion occurred in December 1889 when Reginald junior married Fanny Berkeley Calcott at St Peter's, Oundle. Like his father, Reginald junior was ordained.

The man who emerges from the pages of the early magazines is sincere, hard-working and generous, with strong Christian convictions. He was a true father of his flock, typifying what we think of as Victorian virtues. It was a very different parish from the one we know today – not only smaller but with a very different social mix. Today it is a mainly commuter village with a definite middle class bias, but in the late-Victorian period the majority of inhabitants were framework knitters, farm labourers and domestic servants, with only a minority of professionals and businessmen. These latter provided the churchwardens, ran the societies and, most importantly, funded all of the good causes, but it was the poorer majority (and there was some real poverty) to whom Reginald wrote his letters and gave his care. Of course, there were many in the village who attended the other churches, or were untouched by religious beliefs, but he regarded himself as a friend to all.

His own Christian convictions were made plain in his letters, but he did not confine himself to religious topics. He was a strong advocate of the virtue of thrift. In his very first letter he wrote:

You will have noticed that by arrangements with the central authorities, our Post Office has now become a Money Order Office, and a Savings Bank. I am pleased to find that many have availed themselves of the facilities of getting Money and Postal Orders so near at hand, instead of having to go to Carlton or Lowdham to procure them. I should have been glad if a greater number of Savings Bank accounts had been opened. It is impossible that anyone can doubt the necessity of putting by something when in good work against the time, which always arrives some day or other, when trade is dull and work scarcer. No greater or easier opportunities of putting into any Savings Bank can be given than are afforded at our parish Post Office. You have no distance to go to it, for it is close at hand for all of you. You cannot make a mistake in the day, for it is open every day. You need not wait until you have any large sum to put in, as they will take a shilling at a time. And, remember, no bank can be safer, because, both your money and your interest are secured by Government. I hope for your own comfort you will make use of this Savings Bank, and encourage your children also to begin the habit of putting by a little, instead of spending every penny as soon as they get it.

Temperance was also a cause he had greatly at heart, and he encouraged membership of the Church of England Temperance Society and its juvenile branch. In February 1894 he reported:

Temperance Tea

On Tuesday, January 2nd, a hundred and seven Members of the Juvenile Branch of the Church of England Temperance Society met for their annual tea. After a very merry tea some of the Members gave recitations and some hymns were then thrown on the sheet and sung: after this, the following stories were illustrated by slides: The Wreck of the Hesperus, Dotheboys Hall, The Adventures of Mr. Snap Shot, The History of a Bicyclist.

This gives a typical account of the kind of entertainment popular at the time: each of the organizations had an annual tea in January followed by an unsophisticated entertainment such as is described. In December 1885 he wrote more seriously about carol singing by the choir boys:

But I should be neglecting a present duty if I did not say that complaints from the parents of some of the boys reached me last Christmas-time showing that what should be improving may be hurtful. They said that their children, on returning home, bore only too evident traces of having been treated to what had done them harm instead of good.

A moment's consideration would prevent any one from contributing to such an unhappy result.

In theory we are all anxious to be looked upon as advocates of the Temperance cause to which our carol-singers are pledged. In practice let us, at least, show our consistency by helping and not hindering it.

Let me entreat you, if your generosity be shown in other ways than by gift of money, to let any refreshment offered to these boys be of a character which will not intoxicate.

Reginald was concerned with the improvement of both body and mind, and was instrumental in setting up the Men's Reading Room in the Carnarvon Rooms, the original school, which had become available. In March 1894 he presented the idea:

I have long wished to see a suitable Reading Room for working men in our Parish . . . the scheme, if carried out in its entirety, will give a room for reading and games, and a small room opening from it . . . in order that those who prefer reading in quiet may do so. It will also provide a third room . . . available for . . . meetings and classes in connection with the work of the church.

Donations were rapidly received and a successful bazaar raised the balance. The reading room was opened in December 1894. It served his twin ideals of self-improvement and temperance since it provided a social centre apart from the public houses. It was popular, as the *Weekly Express* reported:

There is a capital billiard table and other games, such as chess, draughts, and dominoes may also be enjoyed in the recreation room, a smaller room being set apart for reading. It is well furnished and lighted, and the

Reginald Ward Thompson (in the boater) with his cricket team, The Harvesters, outside the old vicarage, 1889

fifty members who now enjoy the use of it are much indebted to Mr.
Thompson, the vicar, and the other gentlemen who took an active part
in the promotion of the little institution.

Practical improvements to the village were also supported. Reginald wrote
in 1885:

We were much struck on our visit to Lowdham at seeing the village
furnished with lamps in the streets. This public convenience is an
arrangement which any one passing through Burton Joyce on a dark
night must wish to see soon adopted here.

Accompanying the following sad notice in November 1888 he wrote at
length:

Burials

Sept. 29. – Arthur Dring, aged 7.
October 7. – Beatrice Ethel Perry, aged 7.
     ”   12. – Sidney Smith, aged 9 (at Nottingham).
     ”   20. – Leonard Cragg, aged 10.

My good Friends,
Since the last Magazine was in your hands, our Parish has been subject
to a sad visitation of sickness.

In several instances households in our midst have been rendered
desolate by some who are near and dear to them being taken away.
Many more have been disquieted and distressed by anxiety on behalf of
those among them being stricken down.

It is, indeed, a sad and sorrowful thing; every parent knows how sad
and sorrowful it is, to lose any of the children given to them by God.

One part of our duty in so living is to see that, in so far as lies in our
power, we do good and avoid doing harm, either spiritually or bodily to
our neighbours.

We cannot carry out our duty as regards their bodily condition, if we
allow anything to exist which is harmful to their health. And, practically,
we must be doing them harm if we allow any offensive and
unwholesome matter to accumulate near to them.

I am led to refer to this subject because the Medical Officer of Health
has lately paid several visits to our village. He is an intelligent and zealous
man; and he tells me that there are, in this place, many foul spots which

would certainly spread, if they did not even breed, disease.

This ought not to be, for God, who gave us common sense, gave it to us that we might make use of it.

And I want you to do your best, not only in removing any such foul spots as exist, but in taking care that no fresh ones are created in our village.

You know what I mean.

We cannot be too particular in not allowing unwholesome matter to accumulate in any one spot.

You should all be very careful in seeing that what goes into your drains has free course to run away.

If the drains near you are choked or broken, that means danger. If you will report any such case to me, I will at once let the Medical Officer know about it, and he will gladly attend to it.

You should never allow any collection of vegetable matter to decay near your houses.

Seeing to these things is not a business of any one class or one person amongst us. Everyone is concerned in that business; everyone, even the poorest of us, can help or hinder in that way.

See that you help, and do not hinder. And do your best to make our Parish a wholesome and healthy place, in which to spend such time here as God may grant to us.

Yours sincerely,

REGINALD W. THOMPSON.

A permanent reminder of Reginald Thompson's years as vicar is to be found in the east window of St Helen's. He instigated the idea, organized the raising of funds and approached the artist Kempe to design the window, which was installed and dedicated in July 1888, together with a memorial window to his daughter Edith Elizabeth.

He was also a member of the Land and Building Society started by Mr Roberts, which at this time was developing St Helen's Grove.

Thompson was no narrow-minded killjoy. He was an enthusiastic cricket supporter, regularly reporting on the local team's activities and running his own team, The Harvesters. He was always glad to report on any entertainments being organized in the village. Miss Winifred Blagg, writing in the 1960s of her memories of him, comments that Miss Maud Thompson was in advance of her time in having the GFS girls for games on Saturday afternoons, and the 'big' girls for tennis in the evenings.

That Thompson himself was in advance of his time in his attitude to other denominations is shown in a letter of January 1893:

MY GOOD FRIENDS,

In looking over a German Kalendar recently, I was much struck by a particular feature which I found in it.

Those kinsmen of ours, the Germans, are divided, you know, as in their form of religion into those who are Romanists and those who are members of the Reformed Churches.

Well, I found in their Kalendar that the two branches of Christians in Germany had, for every day in the year save one, a different Saint whom they commemorated. But on that one day, *New Year's Day*, both branches of the Church in that country had the same name entered in the Kalendar as that to be commemorated.

And that name was JESUS.

Now we know that there are differences of ideas among Christians as to some points of doctrine or observances. But do not the facts to which I have alluded show us clearly that there can be no difference of opinion between any and all of us as to who shall be our real head and Master, as to who is the source and beginning of all things which work together for our good, JESUS CHRIST, OUR LORD?

During his twenty years as vicar, Reginald worked conscientiously, running the church services, keeping the church in repair, organizing classes and societies, ably helped by his wife and daughter. He had the satisfaction of seeing the numbers attending Easter Communion steadily grow and of being held in respect and affection by the people of the two villages.